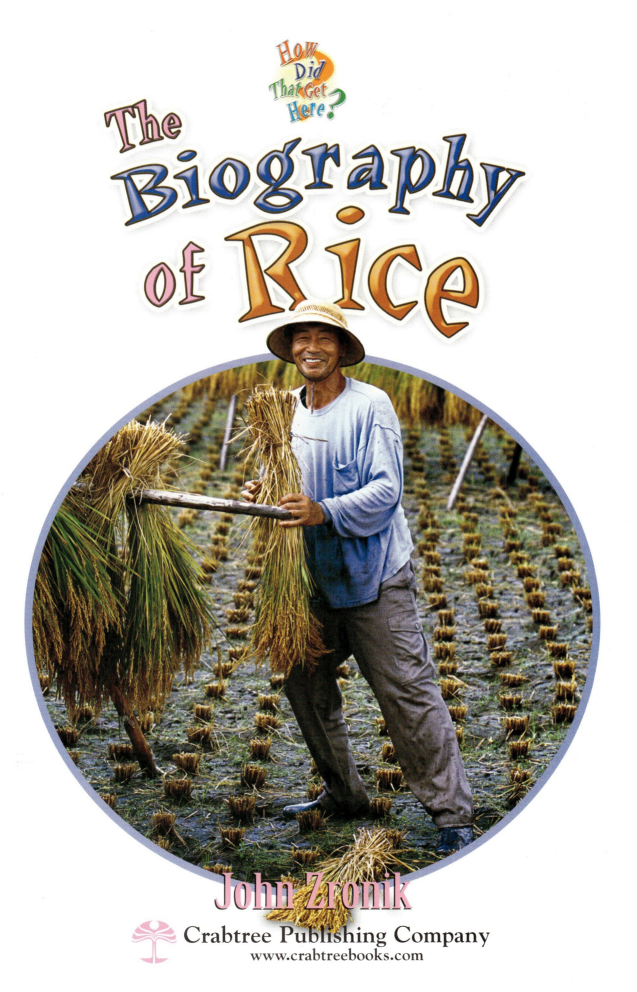

How Did That Get Here?

The Biography of Rice

John Zronik

Crabtree Publishing Company
www.crabtreebooks.com

Crabtree Publishing Company
www.crabtreebooks.com

To my mom, for all her love and support

Coordinating editor: Ellen Rodger
Series editor: Carrie Gleason
Project editor: Rachel Eagen
Editors: Adrianna Morganelli, L. Michelle Nielsen
Production coordinator: Rosie Gowsell
Production assistance: Samara Parent
Art direction: Rob MacGregor
Scanning technician: Arlene Arch-Wilson
Photo research: Allison Napier

Consultant: Jim Fitch, Director, The Rice Museum, Georgetown, South Carolina

Photo Credits: AP/ Wide World Photos: p. 30 (bottom); The Art Archive/ Oriental Art Museum Genoa/ Dagli Orti: p. 11; The Art Archive/ Tokyo University/ Laurie Platt Winfrey: p. 13 (bottom); Private Collection/ Bridgeman Art Library: p. 18; Paul Almasy/ Corbis: p. 20, p. 21 (top); Adrian Arbib/ Corbis: p. 5 (bottom); Tony Arruza/ Corbis: p. 22 (both), p. 23; Bettmann/ Corbis: p. 15; Corbis: p. 16; Robert Essel NYC/ Corbis: p. 1; Jack Fields/ Corbis: p. 30 (top); Mark E. Gibson/ Corbis: p. 31 (top); Richard Glover/ Corbis: p. 21 (bottom); Bob Krist/ Corbis: p. 19 (bottom); Carl & Ann Purcell/ Corbis: p. 8;

Reuters/ Corbis: p. 25 (bottom), p. 26, p. 28 (bottom), p. 31 (bottom); Anders Ryman/ Corbis: p. 24; Phil Schermeister/ Corbis: p. 5 (top); Lee Snider/ Photo Images/ Corbis: p. 19 (top); Ted Spiegel/ Corbis: p. 27 (bottom), p. 29; Keren Su/ Corbis: p. 9 (bottom); Jim Sugar/ Corbis: p. 27 (top); Philip Wallick/ Corbis: p. 13 (top); Simon Oxley/ istock International: p. 9 (top); Suzannah Skelton/ istock International: p. 7 (top left, top right, bottom left, bottom right); North Wind Picture Archives: p. 14, p. 17; Chris Stowers/ Panos Pictures: p. 25 (top), 28 (top); Steve Vidler/ Superstock: cover. Other images from stock cd.

Illustrations: Rob MacGregor: p. 6

Cartography: Jim Chernishenko: p. 10

Cover: Women in Nepal separate rice from bits of husk and bran through a process called winnowing.

Title page: A rice worker hangs harvested rice plants upside-down so they can dry out before processing.

Contents: Rice is eaten by over half of the world's population every day.

Crabtree Publishing Company
www.crabtreebooks.com   1-800-387-7650

Cataloging-in-Publication Data
Zronik, John Paul, 1972-
    The biography of rice / written by John Zronik.
       p. cm. -- (How did that get here?)
    ISBN-13: 978-0-7787-2482-7 (rlb)
    ISBN-10: 0-7787-2482-4 (rlb)
    ISBN-13: 978-0-7787-2518-3 (pbk)
    ISBN-10: 0-7787-2518-9 (pbk)
  1. Rice--Juvenile literature. I. Title. II. Series.
    SB191.R5Z76 2005
    633.1'8--dc22
                                             2005019021
                                             LC

Published in the United States
PMB 16A
350 Fifth Ave.
Suite 3308
New York, NY
10118

Published in Canada
616 Welland Ave.
St. Catharines
Ontario, Canada
L2M 5V6

Published in the United Kingdom
73 Lime Walk
Headington
Oxford
OX3 7AD
United Kingdom

Published in Australia
386 Mt. Alexander Rd.
Ascot Vale (Melbourne)
VIC 3032

Contents

A Global Food Staple

Rice is an edible grain eaten by more than half of the world's population every day. It is also the world's third largest crop, behind corn and wheat. Rice is a cereal crop. Other examples of cereal crops are oats, barley, wheat, and rye. Rice is eaten plain, combined in dishes such as soups and casseroles, and is also used to make products such as paper, glue, flour, noodles, and baby foods.

In the Past

Historians believe rice has been **cultivated** in Southeast Asian countries, including China, Thailand, and Burma, for about 7,000 years. Rice and other grains are important because they can be stored for long periods of time without spoiling. Ancient peoples relied on rice for food during the winter months, when the frozen fields could not be used to grow crops.

Rice as a Commodity

Rice is called a food staple, because it is the main food eaten in many countries. In Japan, China, Thailand, and India, rice is often eaten at every meal. Rice was slowly introduced as a food crop in Europe, North and South America, and Australia over thousands of years of trade and wars. Today, rice is a global commodity, or good that is bought and sold on a world market.

Rice Families

Most rice plants are grown in flooded fields called paddies. Some rice, called dryland rice, needs little water to grow. Floating rice is grown in deep water. There are two main families of rice, Asian and African rice. There are thousands of rice varieties within these two families. The botanical, or scientific, name for Asian rice is *Oryza sativa*. The botanical name for African rice is *Oryza glaberrima*.

▼ *In Japan, the word for meal,* **gohanmono,** *means "honorable cooked rice."*

A Rice that is not a Rice

In North America, people grow and eat a seed that comes from a wild grass called *Zizania aquatica*. The plant is commonly called wild rice, even though it is a vegetable, and is not a true rice. Wild rice grows in regions of Canada, including the Great Lakes region and the province of Saskatchewan. It is also grown in Minnesota, Wisconsin, and California. Wild rice seeds are from 0.5 to three inches (one to seven centimeters) long, and range from light to dark brown in color. Wild rice has a chewy texture.

(right) Wild rice is traditionally harvested by hand by people in canoes, but today it is more commonly harvested by machines.

(above) These rice farmers are tending the fields in a rice paddy. In some African and Asian countries, people depend on rice as their only regular and reliable source of food.

What is Rice?

There are thousands of varieties of rice, which came about because of differences in climate and growing conditions around the world. Rice is classified according to size, shape, color, and texture. All varieties of rice have the same **biological** parts.

Parts of the Plant

Rice plants are long, thin plants that look like tall blades of grass. The head of the plant is called the panicle. It grows at the top of the plant's stalk, above long, flat green leaves. Small flowers called spikelets sprout from the panicle. The spikelets ripen and dry out over several months, eventually producing over 100 tiny grains of rice. Rice plants grow for three to seven months before they are harvested.

Inside the Grain

Each grain of rice is encased in a strong outer shell, called a hull or husk. A layer of bran is beneath the hull. This protective bran layer can be light brown, black, or red in color, depending on the variety. The bran layer contains fiber, protein, and **minerals**. The aleurone layer is a thin layer of **cells** that is found beneath the bran layer. The aleurone layer covers the endosperm, which is the **starchy** part that people eat. The endosperm provides nourishment, or food, to the germ, or seed of the rice plant, while it is growing. The endosperm is high in **carbohydrates**, which all living things need for energy.

Rice plants grow between three to six feet (one to two meters) tall, depending on the species and climate in which they grow. When the plants turn golden yellow, they are ready to be harvested.

Long, Medium, and Short

Rice is classified into three categories: long grain, medium grain, and short grain. Long grain rices are about three times longer than they are wide. Medium grain rices are about twice as long as they are wide. Short grain rices are only slightly longer than they are wide, and are almost round in shape.

(above) Uncooked short grain brown rice.

Sticky and Waxy

Sticky, or waxy, are terms used to describe rice that contains small amounts of a starch called amylose. These rices absorb less water than nonwaxy rices while they are cooking, and feel sticky or gluey when they are ready to eat.

(top) Long grain brown rice.

(middle) Sticky rice is used to make sushi.

What's the Difference?

Rices vary in nutritional value as well as in color, shape, and texture. Brown rices, which are sold with the bran layer intact, are higher in minerals, such as calcium, iron, and protein, than rice that is sold without the bran layer.

The bran layer is removed from rice through processes called husking, milling, and polishing. People need minerals to stay healthy. For this reason, it was believed for many years that brown and black rices were healthier to eat than white rices. **Nutritionists** have recently found that it is difficult for people to digest the bran layer, so the extra minerals in brown rices are not absorbed by the body.

(right) Himalaya red rice comes from the Himalaya Mountains in Asia.

(left) Short grain black rice turns purple when it is cooked.

Growing Rice

Rice is grown from seeds, or grains of rice that are still in the outer hull. Rice seeds are soaked in water for 24 hours before planting. During this time, the grains soften and sprout small green shoots. The seeds are then planted in fields. Some farmers plant the seeds in nursery beds, which are smaller plots of soil where the seedlings are carefully tended to while they are growing. Rice seedlings are transplanted, or moved, to larger fields once they have developed a root system. This takes about 30 days.

Photosynthesis

Like all green plants, rice develops through a process called photosynthesis. During photosynthesis, the roots of rice plants draw up **nutrients** and water from the soil. At the same time, the leaves of the plants absorb sunlight with the help of a green **pigment** called chlorophyll. The leaves also absorb carbon dioxide, a gas that humans breathe out. The combination of sunlight, carbon dioxide, and water and nutrients from the soil, allows a chemical reaction to take place. The chemical reaction produces sucrose, a sugar that provides food for the plant and gives it energy to grow.

Irrigated Rice

Wet rice cultivation is also known as irrigated rice farming, because the crop is grown with large amounts of water. Farmers carefully monitor the water levels in their fields. Bunches of two to six seedlings are pushed into the soil, and the fields, or paddies, are then flooded with water. Low mud walls, called dikes, surround the fields to keep the water inside the paddies. The fields are drained at harvest time. Rice is grown this way in parts of Vietnam, China, Thailand, Italy, Spain, Japan, the United States, and Australia.

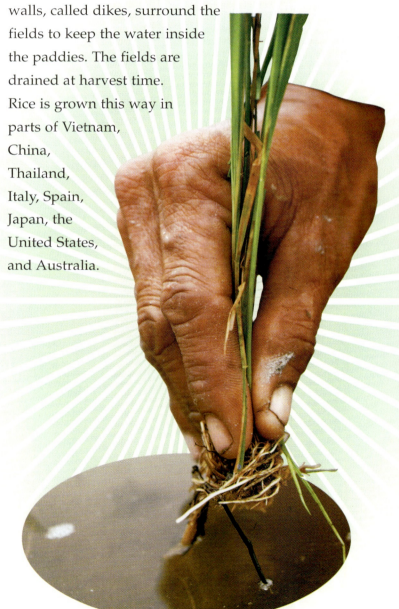

▶ *Rice seedlings are planted once they have developed a root system.*

Dryland Rice

Dryland rice describes rice crops that depend on rainfall to nourish the plants. The fields are not flooded, or irrigated, so farmers have to rely on the weather to keep the crops watered. Dryland rice is sometimes planted along riverbanks, where the soil is moist, or on flat **lowlands**. Dryland fields are found in parts of Southeast Asia and Africa, where there is a rainy season. The seedlings are usually planted just before the rains start in May, and are ready for harvesting as the rains die down, in September. Dryland rice farmers also build earthen dikes around the fields to keep the soil moist.

Floating Rice

Some rice varieties are grown in water up to six feet (two meters) deep. These varieties are usually grown in countries that experience **monsoon** rains. The rice seeds are planted along riverbanks when the water level is at its lowest. As the rains begin, the water level of the river rises. The rice grows at the same speed as the rising waters, so that the panicles, or heads of the plants, remain above the water. By the time the rains stop, the plants are in deep water, and the ripened rice appears to be floating on top. In some places, floating rice is harvested by people in boats. Floating rice is grown in the Niger River in Mali, Africa, and in the large river deltas of Asia.

(top) Rice seedlings are kept in nursery beds for about 30 days before they are planted in fields.

(left) Irrigated rice can be grown on terraces, or platforms, cut into the sides of steep mountains.

Rice Lands

Historians believe that rice cultivation began around 7,000 years ago in the region of Asia that stretches across the south of China to Burma, Thailand, and Assam, India. Rice eventually spread to other parts of Asia, including Japan, Indonesia, and more areas in India. The wet monsoon rains that fall from May to September make these countries ideal for growing rice. Rice farmers in Asia still depend on the summer rains for a successful crop. In cooler, **temperate** regions, rice matures less rapidly because there is not as much water to nourish the plants.

A Monsoon Crop

Climate plays a large role in how rice grows. Rice matures more quickly in warm, **tropical** regions, especially where monsoon rains fall for almost half of the year. A monsoon is an enormous mass of air that blows in one direction during the winter, making the land hot and dry. The wind shifts to blow in the opposite direction during the summer, bringing heavy rains. Asian farmers grow about 90 percent of the world's rice. Without the annual wet season, half the population of Asia would starve.

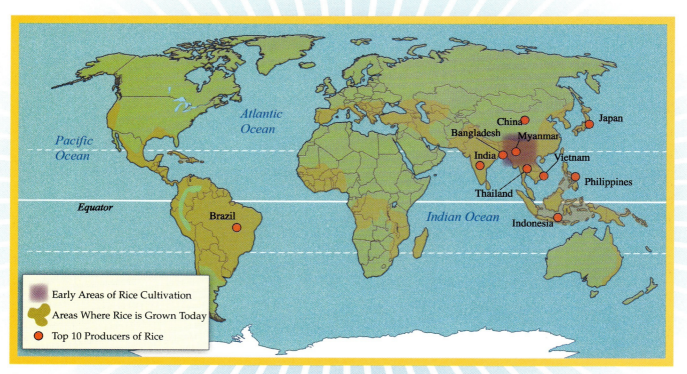

Four-hundred million tons (362,873,896 tonnes) of rice are eaten around the world every year. In Asia, each person consumes an average of more than 176 pounds (80 kg) a year. People eat much less rice in the United States, about 20 pounds (nine kilograms) each year.

Beyond Asia

Over thousands of years, rice cultivation spread out to other parts of the world. Today, rice is grown in Africa, Australia, Europe, South America, and the United States. In the United States, rice is grown in Arkansas, northern California, Louisiana, Mississippi, Missouri, Florida, and Texas. The United States **exports** much of the rice it produces. It is sold in countries that cannot meet their own demand for rice, or do not have the proper climate to grow it.

(background) Rice has been an important crop in Asia since ancient times. This painting shows people planting rice seedlings in Japan, during heavy summer rains.

The Spread of Rice

Around 7,000 years ago, the people of Southeast Asia planted rice on the edges of riverbanks or on wet valley floors. The earliest varieties grown were long and medium grain rices. The grain provided food, while the stalks and leaves of the plant were woven to make shoes, mats, and roofs for houses.

Early Cultivation

Over time, people learned that flooding the rice fields prevented them from drying out under the hot sun, and helped control weeds. At this time, people also ate wild plants and fruits because they could not yet cultivate rice on a large scale. As people spread out to **forage** for food, they also spread their techniques for growing and harvesting rice. Rice farming spread to Vietnam, the Malay Peninsula, and the Philippines around 3000 B.C., and arrived in India around 2400 B.C.

Rice Villages

Rice farmers in Asia began carving long, wide steps into the sides of mountains. This created terraces, or platforms, that were used to grow rice on steep mountain slopes. A series of canals directed rain runoff to the terraces, and drained excess water away after heavy storms. Earthen walls kept some of the water within the paddy walls. As rice farming became more sophisticated, populations increased, and people began settling in permanent villages that centered around growing rice. Work was organized so that everyone in the village took part in producing the crop.

Rice terraces maximized the amount of land that could be used for growing food, and could feed more people.

The Silk Road

Around 200 A.D., merchants traveled and traded with each other along a network of routes and canals known as the Silk Road. The routes connected China to the Middle East, a region bordering the southern and eastern shores of the Mediterranean Sea. Asian merchants traded tea, silk, and spices in exchange for gold, silver, and gemstones from the Middle East along these routes. Asian traders also brought rice and techniques for cultivating the crop to the Middle East, where it became a central part of people's diets.

Rice in Europe and Africa

Rice came to Europe around 600 A.D. At this time, **Arabs** from the Middle East were conquering parts of what is now northern Africa, Italy, Spain, and Portugal. Wars were fought between the Arabs, who followed the religion of **Islam**, and the Europeans, who were **Christians**. The two sides fought for control over land. Invading armies from the Middle East brought their love of rice, as well as their knowledge of how to cultivate it. The Arabs were eventually driven out of Europe, but their techniques for growing rice remained in some regions, including Spain. By 1600, rice was grown in Italy and Hungary. Traders also brought rice to the islands of Madagascar and Mauritius, off the east coast of Africa.

A large mechanical harvester cuts ripened rice.

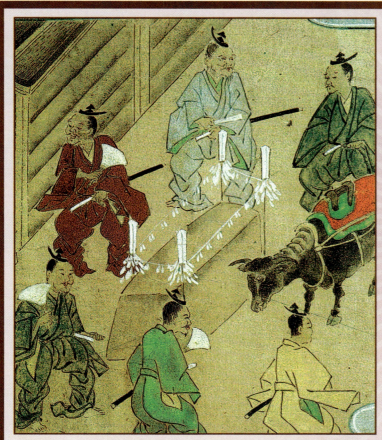

Rice in Japan

Rice cultivation did not spread to Japan until around 200 B.C., when Japan began trading with other Asian countries. Rice quickly became a valuable commodity after it was introduced to Japan. Rice was even used as money. The ancient Japanese did not produce coins because they did not have metal **ores** to make them. Rice was a common item that everyone needed and had access to, so it was used as money instead. When coins were first made by the Japanese, they were difficult to distribute to people who lived high in the mountains. The Japanese continued using rice to pay taxes and wages into the early 1800s.

Rice in the New World

In the late 1400s, European nations were looking to expand their territories by claiming new lands. European kings, inspired by the voyages of explorers such as Christopher Columbus, hired other explorers to find land for settlements in the **New World.**

A slave carries dried rice at harvest time. Most plantations grew only one main crop, such as sugar, spices, or rice.

In the 1500s, the Spanish, Dutch, French, and English built **colonies** in the West Indies, or Caribbean, as well as in parts of North, South, and Central America. The colonists sent large shipments of products from the New World, such as livestock, gold, and food crops, back to Europe, where they were sold in markets.

Rice in the Colonies

The large farms built by colonists were called plantations. In America, rice plantations were built in present-day Georgia and South Carolina by the early 1700s. Rice plantations were also built in present-day Mexico, Brazil, and Peru.

Triangular Trade

Plantation owners needed workers to grow and harvest their crops. At this time, European colonists in the Caribbean and South America imported slaves from West Africa. Slave traders from Europe sailed to Africa's West Coast to trade slaves in exchange for European guns, paper, alcohol, and coins. In Africa, some rulers had slaves for their own plantations and other types of work. These slaves came to the New World with knowledge of rice cultivation. Once the slave ships were emptied of their human cargo in the New World, they were loaded with valuable commodities and sailed back to Europe. The term triangular trade describes the journey that the slave traders traced from Europe, to Africa, to the New World, and back to Europe.

Becoming a Slave

Slave traders docked their ships on the West Coast of Africa, and purchased the slaves of the emperors there. Slave raiders also swept through African villages, stealing people from their homes and families. They were bound with wooden shackles and strung together. Chains of Africans were force-marched to the West Coast, where they were sold into slavery. The slaves were branded on the chest with a symbol that showed who they belonged to. They were then packed into the slave ships and chained together so they could not escape. Disease was rampant because of the filthy and cramped conditions below deck. By the time the ships reached the New World, the slaves were very sick and weak. Many of them died during the voyage.

The New World

In America, slaves were forced onto platforms and sold at auctions. The healthiest and strongest slaves sold for the highest prices. After the sounding of a bell, plantation owners placed signs around the necks of the slaves they had purchased.

Europe-Bound

Once the slave traders had emptied their ships, they used the money they had made from selling slaves to buy large quantities of rice, sugar, rum, molasses, and other foods. The traders then journeyed home to Europe to sell these goods to the very wealthy. The slave traders made a fortune through the slave trade.

Africans were forced onto a platform and sold to plantation owners at slave auctions. Slave traders could charge up to five times more than what they had paid for the slaves in Africa.

Rice Plantations

Rice plantations were first set up in Mexico, Brazil, and Peru. Beginning around 1700, rice plantations were established in the United States. Rice was well suited to the warm weather and marshlands of present-day South Carolina and Georgia. The species grown there was a white rice called Carolina Gold. Rice was also eventually grown in Virginia.

Building a Plantation

Rice planters used slaves to clear large rectangular fields. They chopped or burned down trees to make way for the rice seedlings. Slaves also constructed six-foot (two-meter) mud walls around the marshes to keep the fields flooded. During periods of drought, the fields dried out and were irrigated with water from ditches, which were also dug by slaves. The ditches drained off excess water after very heavy rains. Aside from preparing the land for crops, slaves built their own shelters from pieces of timber. They returned to their quarters at the end of their long days of work.

Daily Drudgery

Rice flourished as a food crop in the United States because of the knowledge and experience brought over by West Africans, who had cultivated it for centuries back home. Most of the slaves who worked in the rice fields were men. Women were sometimes plantation cooks, or maids in the plantation owners' houses. Child slaves tended to the field animals, or helped with the harvest. Slaves worked with simple tools, such as axes, picks, and shovels. Daily meals consisted of boiled grains, such as rice and cornmeal, as well as bacon fat and molasses. Some plantation owners allowed their slaves to tend vegetable gardens, where they grew sweet potatoes and beans. Other slaves improved their diets by eating fish they caught in nearby rivers.

(above) Slaves thresh, or beat, rice with a tool called a flail, to separate the seeds from the straw on a plantation.

Harvest on the Plantation

When the rice was ready for harvesting, slaves cut down the stalks using sickles, or knives with semicircular blades. The stalks were tied together in bundles, then carried away from the field in wagons pulled by mules. At processing barns, slaves hit the bundles with wooden paddles to remove the rice from the stalks. Other slaves ground the grain to remove the husk with wooden mortars and pestles. The rice was then winnowed, or separated from the husk, at a winnowing house, and **sifted** to remove the dust and flour. Finally, the rice was poured through a sieve to separate the whole grains from the broken grains.

Treatment of Slaves

Slaves were forced to work from dawn to dusk in the hot sun. Planting and harvesting required the workers to bend their backs for long periods. The slaves were constantly threatened by the large snakes and alligators that slithered through the paddies. Hard work and **malnutrition** weakened the slaves and made them vulnerable to sicknesses. As many as one-third of the slaves brought to rice plantations in the southern United States died within one year of working.

Against Slavery

Many slaves ran away from the rice plantations, and fled to Canada, where slavery was illegal by 1833. Escaping a plantation was very dangerous. Slaves who were caught running away were dragged back to the plantations, where they were beaten or killed. **Abolitionist** groups were made up of Americans and Europeans who were against slavery. Abolitionists argued that slavery went against basic human rights. The United States became divided between people who opposed slavery and people who supported slavery. In the northern states, most people wanted to outlaw slavery, while in the southern states many people wanted slavery to continue. The two sides fought each other in the American Civil War of 1861 to 1865. The victory of the northern states, backed by the Union Army, in 1865, finally ended slavery in the United States.

▼ *An overseer supervises slaves at work. Slaves who worked too slowly were lashed with a whip or not given food or water.*

End of an Era

The end of the American Civil War in 1865 resulted in the outlawing of slavery in the United States. The war destroyed plantation infrastructure, or processing barns and other facilities, in the southern states. Plantation owners were also without a workforce once the slaves were freed.

Changes in the Fields

Most of the former slaves left the plantations after the war. The end of slavery did not mean that former slaves were completely free. Poverty after the war and **racist** attitudes in parts of the United States made it difficult for former slaves to find work. They were also denied education, and many did not learn important skills such as reading and writing. Rice farmers continued to try to grow rice, but it was difficult to find people to work on the plantations. Frequent storms tore most of the plants out of the soil. Many rice farmers faced **bankruptcy**.

Moving the Rice Fields

In the 1890s, a series of hurricanes and violent storms destroyed the rice fields of South Carolina. This happened around the time when mechanical planters and harvesters were being introduced. Unfortunately, the new machines were too heavy for the soft, wet soil of South Carolina. Rice farming died out in South Carolina in the early 1900s, but soon spread to other areas of the United States, including Arkansas, Louisiana, and Texas, where the land could support the new machines. The machines meant a large work force was no longer needed.

(above) In March 1865, the American government granted all former slaves 40 acres (16 hectares) of farmland, as well as a mule to help them work the land.

18

Rise of the Major Rice Mills

By the early 1900s, large commercial rice mills were established in the southern United States. Shipments of rice were brought to the mills on the Southern Pacific Railroad. The rice was polished by mechanical parts, which ground it against wood or metal drums. The mills were first powered by oxen, and eventually by water. Some of the major rice mills at this time were Georgetown Rice Milling Company, Guendalos Company, and S.M. Ward Company.

This chimney was once part of a rice mill that operated on the Butler rice plantation in Georgia.

Drayton Hall, completed in 1742, is the oldest surviving plantation house in the United States that is open to the public.

Rice Mansions

Plantation owners had enormous houses that were full of expensive furnishings to show off their wealth. After the Civil War, many of these rice mansions were abandoned and fell into disrepair, or were destroyed in storms. Drayton Hall was once home to John Drayton, a rice plantation owner in Charleston, South Carolina. The home is now a fully restored museum. Tourists can visit the building and surrounding grounds to learn about slavery in the South. Visitors can even see copies of documents that show the buying and selling of slaves to and from the Drayton plantation.

Family Farms

In many Asian countries, such as Thailand and Vietnam, most rice is still planted and harvested by hand. Families usually grow and harvest their own supply of rice on small fields no larger than a football field. Most countries have irrigation systems to water their food crops, but in rice-growing areas of India, farmers still depend on the wet monsoon season to nourish the rice crops. During the growing season, the fields must be properly tended. This involves keeping the rice plants free of weeds and disease.

Harvest

On many small rice farms, the rice is still cut using hand-held sickles. It is then hung upside down or laid out in the sun to dry. Farmers then collect the rice into bundles so it can be threshed.

(above) On family rice farms in Asia, everyone has a job. Men prepare fields for planting with the help of plow animals, such as oxen and water buffalo. Women weed and transplant rice seedlings from nursery beds to fields.

Threshing

On small rice farms, threshing is done by hand. Workers bang the rice bundles against a log or mound of earth. Rice at this stage is known as "rough rice" because the grains are still attached to the outer protective husk layer.

Husking and Polishing

The husk and straw of the rice plant are removed before rice is eaten. Traditionally, rice is husked by pounding the grains using a wooden mortar, or bowl, and a pestle. The pestle breaks the hull, and it is removed from the grain by winnowing, or blowing air on the grains. A mortar and pestle are also used to polish, or remove, the bran layer. Some rice is sold, cooked, and eaten with the bran layer still intact.

(left) After it has been harvested, rice is spread out to dry.

Rice in Australia

Japanese politician and businessman Isaburo Takasuka, planted the first rice crop in Australia in 1908. The japonica variety he planted was difficult to grow because of droughts and floods. Takasuka produced a **commercial** crop of rice close to the Murray River in Southeast Australia in 1914. By 1923, new settlers came to the region and also began cultivating rice. Rice continues to be an important crop in this region of Australia, which today is called New South Wales.

Commercial Farms

Today, rice farms in the United States are large, commercial operations. Farmers export their crop to Africa, the Caribbean, Europe, and South and Central America. About 90 percent of the rice crop stays within the United States and is sold in supermarkets. Tractors and other machines are used to plant and harvest the rice, as well as to tend to the growing crop. After harvest, the rice is brought to large mills, where it is processed by other machines.

Planting

Rice fields are planted at the beginning of spring. The fields are first leveled so that the planting surface is flat. Large machines then drill the rice seeds into the soil, or the seeds are dropped into the fields from airplanes. The fields are flooded with water from nearby rivers and canals. Growing rice is kept under two or three inches (five to eight centimeters) of water.

Harvesting the Fields

When the rice is golden and ripe, it is ready for harvest. The fields are drained through a network of canals. Large tractors called combines cut the rice plants at the base of the stalk with large metal blades. The combines then sweep up the stalks and thresh the grains from the stalk. The rice is brought to drying rooms, where warm, dry air removes the field moisture from the rice. The rice is then processed at a mill.

(top, right) Threshed rice is delivered into a bin.

(bottom, right) A modern rice mill in Florida.

Milling

Dried rice is shipped to large processing plants called mills, where it is husked and polished by machines. Here, the rough rice passes through rubber rollers that crack the rice husk. Large fans winnow, or blow away, the husks. The rice is then polished using machines that grind the grains until the white endosperm and germ are exposed. Rice is sorted according to quality. Broken or discolored rice is not packaged for sale in supermarkets.

Parboiling

Some rice is parboiled. Parboiling is a process that partially cooks rice using steam pressure. Rice is parboiled before it is husked and polished. Hot jets of steam force some of the nutrients from the bran and husk into the rice grain. Parboiled rice looks slightly yellow in comparison to white rice. Thailand produces the most parboiled rice. It is exported to countries in Europe, the Mediterranean, South Africa, and the Middle East.

(below) Massive modern combine tractors cut and thresh rice today in one step.

The Culture of Rice

Rice production has shaped people's lives for thousands of years. In many countries, a plentiful rice crop ensures that people will not starve. In Bali, Indonesia, ceremonies mark the planting season, when people bring rice seedlings from nursery beds to fields.

Rice Shrines

The people of Bali were once plagued with terrible famines. According to legend, the Balinese were saved from starvation when the gods made rice grow in their fields. To show their gratitude, the Balinese now build **shrines** in their rice fields for the goddess of fertility and agriculture, Dewi Sri. The people of Bali believe that offerings to their most beloved goddess will please her and ensure a plentiful harvest.

The Rice Dog

In China, people tell many stories about how rice came to their country. One story tells about a flood that swept over the land and forced people to flee their homes. When the flood waters subsided, people returned home to find that their crops had been ruined. The people suffered until one day, a dog came wandering into the village with yellow seeds hanging from his tail. The people took the seeds and planted them. Rice sprouted from the soggy soil, and the people never went hungry again.

Balinese women leave flowers and fruit for Dewi Sri, the goddess of agriculture, in rice paddy shrines built to honor her.

Useful Rice

Rice continues to have a great impact on people's lives in the world today. Rice is used to make baby foods, breakfast cereals, and beer. Starch from rice is used to stiffen clothes, and to make glue and rice vinegar. Rice husks are used in paints, makeup, detergents, soaps, and potting mix for plants. Rice is even used to make alcohol. Sake is a traditional alcoholic drink that the Japanese make from rice.

A man hangs sheets of rice paper in the sun to dry in Nepal. Rice paper is made from rice straw that is chopped, soaked, and cooked. The mixture is then beaten into a pulp and spread out in sheets.

Working in Rice

Rice farming continues to be labor-intensive, requiring many workers, especially in places where it is cultivated by hand. In many countries, working on rice farms or in rice mills is the main way for people to earn a living. Many rice workers are paid little for their labor. In order for some families to survive, they must send their young children to work on rice farms and mills, rather than attend school. Some women are forced back to work in the fields immediately after childbirth. This can be life threatening. Workers in some countries, such as India, have organized **walk-outs** to protest their poor wages and long work hours, but in many cases, these protests have not changed anything.

Farmers in South Korea staged a protest to demand fair prices for their rice. The farmers feared that the government would cut the amount of money they paid for rice, reducing farmers' profits.

Rice and the Environment

Growing rice can be both good and bad for the environment. In some ways, rice is an environmentally friendly crop, because little land is needed to produce large amounts of food. There are only small amounts of waste because all parts of the plant are used, either as food, or to make other products.

Locusts are migrating *grasshoppers that descend in large swarms. They destroy rice and other food crops by eating the leaves of the plants.*

Pesticides

Pesticides and insecticides are chemicals that are sprayed on crops to keep away diseases and insects that attack rice crops. Pesticides can help keep insects at bay, but they also contaminate the soil and pollute the local water supply. When the wind blows, small amounts of chemicals from the leaves are carried in the air. This poisoned air is dangerous for humans and animals to breathe. Workers who spray the pesticides are at a higher risk for illnesses, such as cancer.

(above) A plane dusts a rice crop in Texas with pesticides.

Growing Organic

Organic farming is a method of producing food crops without the help of chemical pesticides and **fertilizers**. Organic farmers use natural fertilizers, such as compost and manure. They also grow varieties of rice that are naturally resistant to pests. Scientists are currently studying a variety of rice that contains a natural insecticide. Farmers in China grew the variety on test plots, and found that they used 80 percent less insecticides on their crops than usual.

Greenhouse Gases

The greenhouse effect describes what happens when the sun's heat is trapped by some of the gases in the Earth's **atmosphere**. As the sun shines down on the Earth, heat energy from the sun is absorbed by the surface of the Earth, and is reflected back into the atmosphere. Some gases, called greenhouse gases, trap the heat energy and prevent it from escaping back into the atmosphere. The trapped gases increase the Earth's temperature. This is known as global warming.

Two greenhouse gases are produced by growing rice: nitrous oxide, and methane. Nitrous oxide comes from some of the fertilizers used on rice crops. Methane is released from **organic matter** in the soil, as well as from waste from field animals. Scientists worry that when the Earth gets too warm, the global climate will change and lead to droughts, floods, and heat waves. All of these conditions make it harder to grow rice.

▶ *Rice panicles are examined for disease.*

Engineering Rice

Over half of the world's population relies on rice as a major source of food. Many scientists around the world are trying to develop new strains of rice that are particularly suited to certain climates, or are resistant to common diseases and pests that usually attack crops.

Genetic Modification

The science of improving a crop is called genetic modification. This process involves altering, or changing, rice seeds so that the plants have special characteristics. Through genetic modification, scientists can develop new kinds of rice that look, taste, or grow a certain way.

Miracle Rice

The genetic modification of rice took off in the 1960s and 1970s, when scientists from the International Rice Research Institute (IRRI) in the Philippines developed several new varieties of rice. The new strains were called "miracle rice" because the plants were capable of producing twice as many rice grains than other varieties. The new plants also matured more quickly, allowing farmers to grow up to two rice crops per year.

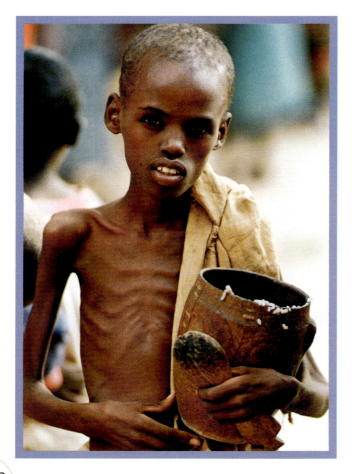

(top) New rice varieties grow in test tubes. Some of the first strains of miracle rice were resistant to drought, so they could be grown in dry climates.

(left) A starving boy clings to a pot of rice. Shipments of rice are sent to famine-struck countries for food relief.

Green Revolution

Miracle rices allowed farmers to grow greater amounts of rice than ever before. This meant that some rice-producing countries did not have to import rice from other countries to feed their population. The period during which miracle rices were developed is called the Green Revolution. This period greatly improved the economies of many countries in Africa and Asia. China and Bali began growing so much rice that they exported some of it to other countries, as well as used it to feed their own populations. Miracle rices can grow in poor soil or drought-prone regions, allowing farmers to grow food on land that was once unsuitable for cultivation.

Drawbacks to Miracle Rice

The Green Revolution helped many rice farmers, but many of the new strains of miracle rice required large amounts of chemical pesticides and fertilizers to stay healthy and grow properly. These chemicals are very expensive, and not all farmers can afford to buy them. Miracle rice also degrades the soil it is grown in. Large irrigation systems, heavy machinery for planting and harvesting, and strong chemicals all put a strain on the land. Over time, the soil becomes exhausted and can no longer support crops, leaving farmers without a source of income, and entire countries without food to eat.

Researchers examine insect-resistant rice plants at the Colombian Institute of Agriculture. Some people are against genetically modified crops because they are grown on such a large, intensive scale that they wipe out biodiversity, or the variety of plants and animals that live in an environment.

The Future of Rice

Rice is one of the most important foods in the world. The work of researchers at the International Rice Research Institute (IRRI) and many other agricultural research organizations has helped farmers produce higher yields with fewer chemicals. The rice varieties that were once cultivated by ancient peoples are no longer grown today.

(right) A Balinese farmer herds a group of ducks into a rice field. Ducks can be used as a natural defense against pests, because they eat insects and leave the rice crop alone.

International Rice Research Institute

IRRI is a nonprofit research organization where scientists work to develop new varieties of rice. Researchers experiment with new seeds, and plant them on IRRI's experimental farm at the University of the Philippines. While the first varieties of miracle rice were considered a breakthrough at the time, scientists are now trying to develop new strains that require less chemicals to grow. They are also trying to develop varieties that can be grown with very little water, so that drought-prone countries can produce food during dry spells.

◄ *Some environmentalists disagree with genetically modified crops because they decrease biodiversity. Some genetically modified crops also require chemicals that are harmful to the surrounding water supply and health of workers.*

STOP THE GENETIC EXPERIMENT
GREENPEACE

Preserving Rice

Newer, high yielding rice varieties have slowly replaced old ones. Scientists need these older varieties in order to continue developing new ones for farmers. A rice genebank at IRRI currently holds about 100,000 different kinds of rice seeds. The genebank is important for maintaining some amount of genetic variety in rice crops. Varieties that are grown on the same plot of land over and over again are extremely vulnerable to disease. Adding some variety to the rice seeds builds the crop's defense against outbreaks of disease.

This rice farmer is checking his crop in California.

Food Security

Food security is a term that describes people having access to the food they need. Growing enough rice to feed the world is less difficult than getting the food to famine-struck regions. Governments around the world can help to improve food security by sending food to countries where drought or pests stop food production.

Rice from this storage facility in Japan is sent to relieve hunger in other countries.

Glossary

abolitionist Someone who fought to end slavery

Arab A person from present-day Saudi Arabia

atmosphere The invisible gases that surround the Earth

bankruptcy The state of having no money

biological The characteristics of a living thing

carbohydrates Energy-producing substances

cells Small units that make up all living things

Christian Followers of the teachings of Jesus Christ

colony Territory ruled by another country

commercial Produced for the sole purpose of making money

cultivate To farm and harvest a crop

export To send a commodity away from the place it was produced, to sell it

fertilizer A substance that helps plants grow

forage To search for food and other supplies

Islam The religion based on the teachings of the prophet Muhammad

lowlands A region of land that lies low and flat, usually between mountain ranges

malnutrition Illness that results from not eating enough healthy foods

migrate To move from one place to another

mineral A natural substance that is usually found under the ground

monsoon An air mass that makes the land hot and dry during the winter, then shifts to bring heavy rains during the summer

New World The name given to North, Central, and South America by Europeans after they discovered that the continents existed

nutrients Substances that all living things need to survive and stay healthy

nutritionist Someone who studies people's diets

ore A valuable substance, such as a metal, that is usually mined from the ground

organic matter Decaying or rotten material

pigment A substance that produces a certain color in a living thing

racism Poor treatment of people because of their race

shrine A place where objects are placed to honor a god or goddess

sift To separate larger particles from smaller ones

starch A substance that stores carbohydrates

temperate A region that has a mild climate and usually several different seasons

tropical A region that has a hot climate with little change between seasons

walk-out A form of protest in which workers leave their place of work

Index

1 2 3 4 5 6 7 8 9 0 Printed in the U.S.A. 4 3 2 1 0 9 8 7 6 5